FEB 2 7 2015

AMAZING FEATS OF

MECHANICAL ENGINEERING

Essential Library

An Imprint of Abdo Publishing | www.abdopublishing.com

MECHANICAL ENGINEERING

by Chris Eboch

Content Consultant

Carrie Hall
Assistant Professor
Illinois Institute of Technology, Chicago

www.abdopublishing.com

Published by Abdo Publishing, a division of ABDO, PO Box 398166, Minneapolis, Minnesota 55439. Copyright © 2015 by Abdo Consulting Group, Inc. International copyrights reserved in all countries. No part of this book may be reproduced in any form without written permission from the publisher. Essential Library™ is a trademark and logo of Abdo Publishing.

Printed in the United States of America, North Mankato, Minnesota
042014
092014

**THIS BOOK CONTAINS
RECYCLED MATERIALS**

Cover Photo: NASA
Interior Photos: NASA, 2, 7, 9, 11, 23, 26, 28, 33, 36, 38 (left), 38 (right), 41; Shutterstock Images, 15, 93; Dorling Kindersley/ Thinkstock, 16; Songquan Deng/Shutterstock Images, 20; Robyn Beck/Getty Images/Newscom, 31; Helen Neafsey/ Greenwich Time/AP Images, 43; Koji Sasahara/AP Images, 45; Keith Srakocic/AP Images, 48; Science Faction/SuperStock/ Glow Images, 53; Liz Hafalia/San Francisco Chronicle/Corbis, 55; Chassenet/BSIP/Corbis, 56; Shamukov Ruslan/ITAR-TASS Photo/Corbis, 59; epa/Corbis, 63; Carolyn Kaster/AP Images, 65; Proehl Studios/Corbis, 67; Stefan Sauer/dpa/Corbis, 72; Per Olofsson/AFP/Getty Images/Newscom, 75; Patrick Pleul/dpa/Corbis, 77; Julia Cumes/AP Images, 80; Patrick Pleul/ picture-alliance/dpa/AP Images, 83; Jens Wolf/EPA/Newscom, 86; Reed Saxon/AP Images, 89; Matt Rourke/AP Images, 95; Nikid Design LTD/DK Images, 96

Editor: Arnold Ringstad
Series Designer: Becky Daum

Library of Congress Control Number: 2014932492

Cataloging-in-Publication Data

Eboch, Chris.
 Amazing feats of mechanical engineering / Chris Eboch.
   p. cm. -- (Great achievements in engineering)
Includes index.
ISBN 978-1-62403-430-5
1. Mechanical engineering--Juvenile literature.   I. Title.
621--dc23

2014932492

Cover: The *Curiosity* rover takes a self-portrait on the Martian surface in this image made up of many stitched-together individual photos.

CONTENTS

CHAPTER 1

CREATING A BETTER WORLD

The scientists of the US National Aeronautics and Space Administration (NASA) held their breath. In August 2012, the Mars rover *Curiosity* had safely completed its eight-month journey through space. But now its capsule had to survive the fall through the Martian atmosphere. In seven minutes, it would need to slow from 13,000 miles per hour (21,000 kmh) to 1.5 miles per hour (2.4 kmh) in order to land without damage. These seven minutes would determine whether *Curiosity* could explore Mars or would smash into its surface. And the whole world was watching.

On average, Mars orbits the sun approximately 50 million miles (80 million km) farther out than Earth.

NASA scientist John Grunsfeld said before the landing, "The *Curiosity* landing is the hardest NASA robotic mission ever attempted in the history of exploration of Mars, or any of our robotic exploration. This is risky business." Some 7,000 people had worked on *Curiosity* over the course of five years. The project cost $2.5 billion.[1] A failure would mean not only the loss of expensive equipment and years of work, but also a tremendous setback to NASA's exploration program. NASA depends on government funding, and expensive failures do not impress the politicians who vote on funding levels.

Steve Sell, the mission's deputy operations lead for entry, descent, and landing, described the arduous preparation phase: "I leave myself voicemails in the middle of the night about things to check in the morning. We've run thousands of tests and simulations, thinking of ways to 'break' the system so we can build in comfortable performance margins. . . . We're always afraid we missed something."[2] A true test of the spacecraft was not possible in Earth's thicker atmosphere and higher gravity, so ultimately the engineers had to have confidence in their design.

The NASA team could not see or hear the descent and landing in real time. It takes 14 minutes for radio signals to travel at the speed of light from Mars to Earth. So by the time the control team learned of any problems, it would be too late to do anything about it. But NASA knew what should happen. The preprogrammed landing process had to be timed perfectly to ensure success. "If any one thing doesn't work just right, it's game over," explained NASA engineer Tom Rivellini.[3]

Friction from the planet's thin atmosphere helped slow the spacecraft to 1,000 miles per hour (1,600 kmh). A heat shield protected the rover from the heat generated by this friction, reaching a temperature of 3,800 degrees Fahrenheit (2,100°C). Then, a 60-foot (18 m) parachute

Curiosity's parachute descent was photographed by another NASA spacecraft already in Martian orbit.

deployed and inflated above the capsule, slowing the capsule to approximately 200 miles per hour (320 kmh).[4] When its job was done, explosive bolts freed the chute. What happened next separated *Curiosity* from all rover landings that came before.

Sky Crane, a jet pack attached to the top of the rover, took over, firing rockets downward and outward to slow the descent even further. The rockets pushed the rover out of the way of its falling parachute. Once its speed dropped low enough to land safely, Sky Crane lowered the rover on three nylon ropes. *Curiosity* dangled 20 feet (6 m) below Sky Crane as it continued to gently fall toward the surface. After the rover touched down, explosive bolts cut the ropes and Sky Crane flew away. Having safely delivered *Curiosity*, it crashed into the ground nearby as planned.

Previous missions had used different landing methods. Some used rockets to lower the spacecraft directly to the surface on a lander with legs. According to NASA engineer Rob Manning, "That's how you're supposed to do it. You're supposed to land with your rocket below you, climb down the ladder, and explore. That's how Buck Rogers did it; that's how the Apollo astronauts did it."[5]

However, the size of the rover, about as big as a compact car, meant the system would be too top-heavy. Other rovers had used airbags,

The Sky Crane system allowed for the most accurate Mars landing in history.

causing them to land, bounce, and gently roll to a stop. This would not have worked for *Curiosity*; again, its size made the scheme too difficult. The NASA team decided to try turning the whole thing upside down, putting the rocket on the roof like a jet pack. "What appears to be a complex system actually simplifies the landing greatly," according to Sell.[6] Still, the system, affectionately called "hope on a rope," did not immediately inspire confidence. Each piece had to be proven through extensive testing, and the landing itself was filled with anxious moments.

Fortunately for NASA, *Curiosity* landed safely. An announcer declared, "Touchdown confirmed. We're safe on Mars," and the mission team erupted in cheers.[7] Such is the life of a mechanical engineer. Hours of careful planning and testing lead to the excitement and drama of waiting to see if a new invention will succeed or fail.

VARIETY AND CREATIVITY

Engineers combine science and math to solve real-world problems and design new products. Different kinds of engineers tackle different problems. Mechanical engineers, who work with machines of all kinds, have perhaps the broadest range of jobs. Their work crosses into computers, automotive technology, and biotechnology. Mechanical engineers might develop children's toys, robots, or life-saving medical devices. They might design car engines, sailboats, or aircraft carriers. If a product involves moving parts, a mechanical engineer was probably involved.

Mechanical engineers can work in a variety of conditions. One may work at a construction site, tackling the challenges of rain, wind, and mud as a new building rises into the sky. Another may work in a spotless lab with microscopic semiconductor parts. A third may work on a computer, writing software simulations to design new products. In each case, the goal is to create new technology and make it work.

The most exciting part of mechanical engineering may be testing a new product. After weeks or months of planning, testing all the parts and ideas, a prototype is built. Will it do everything the engineers want? Will it work at all? So many things could go wrong. The more original the design, the more room there is for error. Failure is not the end of the road, but rather one more step in the design process. When everything works, the mechanical engineer has helped make the world a better place.

A GROWING FIELD

The US Bureau of Labor Statistics predicts an increase of nearly 10,000 mechanical engineering jobs in the next few years. Starting salaries average approximately $50,000 per year, while top salaries are more than $100,000.[8] The median annual salary for mechanical engineers is more than $75,000.[9] This is substantially higher than the median salary of $27,500 for all occupations.[10] Mechanical engineers usually enter the workforce with a bachelor's degree. A graduate degree may be needed to get into management or research.

MECHANICAL ENGINEERING

Mechanical engineering focuses on the design, construction, and use of machines. This includes the design and manufacture of everything from small parts to large systems. Whether the object is an ink-jet nozzle or a spacecraft, the mechanical engineer helps shepherd it from idea to product.

Mechanical engineers work on millions of projects in hundreds of fields. The results of mechanical engineering are everywhere. They are in tiny devices and enormous structures, inside our homes and across the globe, and even on other planets. Regardless of the task, one thing is constant—engineers meet unusual challenges that require creative

Mechanical engineers work on projects ranging from the tiny parts inside computers to the enormous components of wind turbines.

thinking. At each stage of development, a fresh idea or a new twist on an old concept can help create something remarkable.

ENGINEERING THROUGH THE AGES

The title *mechanical engineer* has been around for less than two centuries. Yet throughout human history, people have invented and improved upon machines. An object modern people take for granted, such as the wheel, may be the result of thousands of years of innovation. The concept of a wheel started with the use of log rollers to move objects. By 3500 BCE, someone made the leap to using wooden disks attached to a heavy

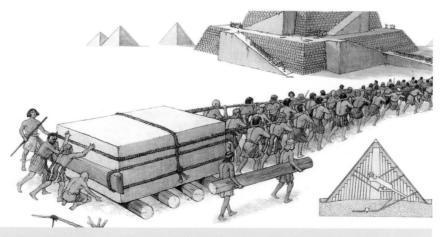

For centuries, the height of transportation technology was the use of logs to move heavy objects.

SCIENCE OR ENGINEERING?

For much of human history, science and engineering were seen as very different disciplines. Scientists focused on understanding how the natural world works. They often avoided experimentation or practical inventions. Meanwhile, the goal of engineering is to create technology that benefits humanity. Engineers built buildings, bridges, ships, and labor-saving devices, but they did these things largely without the benefit of scientific knowledge. They depended primarily on trial and error.

Science and engineering met during the Renaissance, which began in the 1300s. Both disciplines benefited. If a bridge failed or a ship sank, scientists and engineers would work together to apply scientific lessons from the disaster to future engineering projects. Today, engineering is founded on science. Scientists and engineers work closely together. Sometimes their methods are indistinguishable.

sled. Some 1,500 years later, another inventor replaced this with spokes attached to an outer rim. Later advances included new materials, such as metal spokes and rubber tires. As wheels became more varied and common, they allowed people to use animal, water, and wind power. People could do more with less physical work. Early carts pulled by people or animals led to automobiles, bicycles, trucks, and trains. Each of these advances required mechanical engineers.

The common saying "Necessity is the mother of invention" is a good mantra for mechanical engineering. Difficult situations encountered in everyday life inspire ingenious solutions. A new invention may lead to other improvements to the surrounding world. When they wanted to get the most out of the wheel as a transportation device, people built roads. Traces still remain of Roman stone roads built across Europe more than 2,000 years ago. Today some of these road fragments lie not far from high-speed highways and workshops where companies are designing the latest automobiles.

Roads and the vehicles that travel on them still help move people and goods. Wheels also allow people to explore the world. They even find use on other worlds, as on *Curiosity*. A simple, practical solution to a basic transportation problem led to places those early inventors could not have imagined.

Once an idea is in use, it tends to lend itself to other applications. Wheels are no longer simply practical devices; they are now used for fun on in-line skates and skateboards. Airplanes use wheels not only to move across the ground, but also as rotors in their engines. The wheel's rolling motion makes it possible to have gears, pulleys, bearings, and other machine parts. Compact discs use the spinning motion of a wheel, too. The basic concept may be thousands of years old, but today's engineers use the wheel in creative new ways. Mechanical engineers helped make the wheel the versatile and valuable tool it is today. They will continue to find new uses and improvements, including some we cannot yet imagine.

SURVIVAL AND COMFORT

The devices created by engineers do far more than help people travel and explore. They help people survive. Centuries ago, well-engineered walls and fortresses helped keep out enemies. Today, cozy, heated homes provide protection from the elements. Running water and refrigeration make for more sanitary living conditions. This helps people stay healthy and contributes to a more pleasant life.

Engineers help with human survival in other ways as well. Ultrasound machines and other medical devices help diagnose diseases. Robotic surgery systems are among the many devices doctors use to treat patients. Meanwhile,

STRONGER AND TALLER

For thousands of years, people built buildings primarily from wood or stone. New methods of making iron developed during the Industrial Revolution and provided a stronger building material. This allowed engineers to design larger structures, such as the 1889 Eiffel Tower in Paris, France. Further advances in making steel from iron enabled engineers to build skyscrapers. But skyscrapers required another invention to be practical: the elevator. New materials, such as concrete reinforced with steel, provided new construction options, making possible buildings of 100 stories or more. The advances continue today, with innovations allowing stronger, lighter, more efficient buildings.

The lighted city skylines of today would not be possible without the innovations made by mechanical engineers over the last few centuries.

prosthetic limbs, pacemakers, and artificial heart valves help injured or sick people live normal lives.

Many of the inventions of the last century require sources of electricity. In our homes and businesses, lights, heaters, refrigerators, computers, and many more items need power. Producing energy has been one of the great challenges of engineering in the last century. The focus today is on developing clean and efficient energy sources. This is partly required to combat the pollution released from the production and use of earlier products designed by mechanical engineers.

Advances in engineering can do damage despite their advantages. Cars allow people great freedom of movement, but they also release exhaust that pollutes the environment. Modern engineers look for ways to reduce the environmental impact of their inventions. Many work on improving current designs so they are safer, healthier, or more efficient.

From medical devices to the energy industry to vehicles and tools of all kinds, mechanical engineering helps people survive, travel, enjoy life, and explore the universe.

THE ROAD TO MARS

The *Curiosity* Mars rover is one of the most impressive feats of modern engineering. *Curiosity* was not the first rover to land on Mars, but it was by far the biggest. Its goal was to gather evidence about the possibility Mars once had life. Evidence of life on Mars would prove we are not alone in the universe. Doug McCuistion, director of Mars exploration at NASA headquarters, said the mission "could arguably be the most important event in the history of planetary exploration. It truly is a major step forward, both in technology and in potential science return."[1]

Developing the rover and its spacecraft presented a huge engineering challenge.

WHY MARS?

Mars is of special interest to scientists because of its similarity to Earth. Mars is now dry and cold, but it may have had conditions more like Earth in the past. Missions to Mars attempt to understand the history of climate and water on the planet. In particular, they look for conditions that may once have hosted living things. Mars rovers use scientific instruments to read the geologic record at different sites. This record might show whether conditions on Mars could have allowed living creatures to develop.

Life as we know it cannot exist without organic molecules. These molecules contain carbon atoms bound to other elements. Other elements, such as oxygen, nitrogen, phosphorus, and sulfur, are also important for life. If Mars exploration detects these ingredients on Mars, there may be a greater chance life existed there.

Many challenges exist in exploring Mars. Depending on its position in orbit, Mars is anywhere from 33.9 million miles (54.6 million km) to 249 million miles (401 million km) away from Earth.[2] The journey between the planets takes months. During the flight, thrusters are used to adjust the spacecraft's direction. This process must be carefully planned in order to reach Mars. And getting there is only the beginning. A rover must fall through the Martian atmosphere at high speed and land safely. Then it must travel across the uneven landscape. It must deploy its equipment, take samples and photographs, and send information millions of miles through space back to Earth. Finally, the rover must have a steady source of power throughout the mission, as there is no way to add fuel or replace batteries.

STEP BY STEP

The first step in engineering is to define the problem and identify the goal. According to NASA, *Curiosity*'s goal was not to look for life. Instead, scientists designed the rover to look for areas that could have been favorable for life in the past. If appropriate areas were found, the discovery would shape future missions to bring back samples to Earth. *Curiosity* landed in a region already known to have once had water, a key requirement for life to exist. Several other factors are believed to be necessary for life. Life needs a source of energy, which could include heat from the sun. It also requires certain chemical ingredients. Studying Martian soil could tell scientists whether life as we know it could have existed there.

COMMUNICATION PRIORITY

The *Mars Polar Lander* made an unsuccessful attempt at a Mars landing in 1999. Because of the way communication was set up, NASA was unable to get data about what went wrong. NASA then made communication a high priority for future Mars landings. If a lander crashed, NASA wanted to know why so it could adjust plans for future missions. For this reason, during descent and landing, *Curiosity* sent radio transmissions. In case of a landing failure, NASA could learn from the data the rover sent back.

Curiosity's landing site at Gale Crater was chosen because some scientists believed the crater's contents may have been leftover sediment from a lakebed.

Once NASA identified the goals for *Curiosity*, it had to decide how to achieve them. This involves thinking of different designs and whittling them down to a final version. In April 2004, NASA invited researchers to propose science experiments to include on the mission. They selected eight proposals from research centers in the United States and Canada that best contributed to the mission goals. Russia and Spain each provided an additional investigation through international agreements. This process determined the ten science investigations included on *Curiosity*.

Once a company or research group has identified a problem and selected solutions, it needs to build the necessary equipment. Many engineering projects, especially large ones, have teams of engineers, each with its own leader or manager. Different teams are responsible for different parts of the project. Before the overall project is complete, each part must be tested and revised for improvement. When equipment will be used in space, it must have a high probability of working perfectly, since repairs may be difficult or impossible. This requires extensive testing ahead of time.

All engineering projects require testing, but most do not require the engineers to replicate conditions on another planet. As NASA engineer Adam Steltzner says, "Here on Earth, you cannot test one large simulation that takes us from above

TEST AT HOME BEFORE YOU GO

Space agencies prepare for missions by first simulating operations on Earth. Hawaii's volcanic ash deposits provide terrain similar to Mars, the moon, or asteroids. The Arizona desert is another popular spot for field tests. Research teams also conduct tests in specially designed buildings and in computer simulations. These tests help ensure all equipment will work as planned.

Curiosity's parachute is nearly
65 feet (20 m) in diameter.

the atmosphere down to the surface of Mars, not the right atmosphere, not the right gravity."[3] The testing must be broken into pieces and tested in conditions as similar as possible to what will be found on Mars.

Engineer Anita Sengupta developed the design of the enormous parachute that would be used for Curiosity's landing. NASA tested the parachute in a huge wind tunnel. The first test went smoothly, but during the second test, the parachute exploded into pieces. To understand why, the engineers had to re-create the failure so they could capture it on multiple high-resolution cameras. If they did not know why the parachute failed, they could not be sure they would prevent it from happening during *Curiosity*'s landing. Steltzner described the testing process: "And we test again, good chute again; good chute again; and again. And we're like, 'Well, jeez, if we don't see this problem again, it's going to be even worse!' It'd be better to capture it in high resolution, so we can understand what was going on, rather than just have this one-off occurrence."[4]

Finally a parachute exploded. This time they caught it on video. Before inflating fully, one side of the parachute slipped through the lines on the opposite side. This pulled the parachute inside out and tore it apart. But could the same thing happen on Mars? They studied the video for months and finally realized that in the wind tunnel, the parachute took longer to inflate than it would in the Martian atmosphere. The wind tunnel also had gravity pulling the parachute down when it was deployed sideways. These conditions would not happen on Mars, where the parachute would quickly deploy upward. The engineers determined it was an Earth problem, not a Mars problem, and they moved on.

The *Curiosity* teams spent years brainstorming ideas, finding solutions, and testing equipment over and over. All that planning would contribute to the success of *Curiosity*'s mission. The successful landing meant the rover had passed some of the most difficult tests. But would it be able to successfully deploy all its equipment, travel across the surface of Mars, and send back valuable data?

Anita Sengupta is the engineer behind *Curiosity*'s parachute design. While growing up, science fiction characters inspired her, and the vastness of the universe drew her to space exploration. She works for NASA's Jet Propulsion Laboratory in Pasadena, California. As an expert in entry, descent, and landing, she designs systems to land rovers and robots on other planets. These systems may include heat shields, parachutes, and rockets, which work together to safely slow the cargo for landing.

Sengupta led teams of engineers during *Curiosity*'s parachute development phase. NASA scientists, universities, and aerospace corporations worked together on the project. The parachute program took more than four years and included a drop test from a helicopter as well as tests in a supersonic wind tunnel. Sengupta's work directly contributed to *Curiosity*'s successful exploration of Mars. In an interview, she said, "It is hard to put into words what it feels like to accomplish something so difficult. It makes you want to do it all over again, tomorrow."[5]

Sengupta, *right*, took part in a panel discussion about mission with other NASA engineers in August 201

CHAPTER 4

EXPLORING THE RED PLANET

O n the night of August 5, 2012, NASA celebrated *Curiosity*'s successful landing. Yet the team knew many challenges lay ahead. Once a rover arrives on Mars, it must withstand the harsh Martian environment. The temperature ranges from –199 degrees Fahrenheit (–128°C) at the poles to 80 degrees Fahrenheit (27°C) at the equator.[1] The atmospheric pressure on Mars's surface is less than 1 percent of that on Earth.[2] This means some machines will work differently on Mars. Wind speeds are generally low, but wind can gust up to 90 miles per hour (145 kmh), causing dust storms and whirlwinds.[3] Dust storms can cover much of the planet for months, blocking sunlight

NASA engineers celebrated the arrival of the first photos from *Curiosity*. but the rover's work was just beginning.

THE MARTIAN ATMOSPHERE

Liquid water cannot exist on the surface of Mars today. However, geologic evidence suggests that in the past Mars had a different atmosphere and liquid water. The Mars Atmosphere and Volatile Evolution (MAVEN) spacecraft intends to learn more about Mars's climate history. This craft launched into space on November 18, 2013.

MAVEN will not try to land on Mars. Instead, the spacecraft will orbit the planet. Scientific instruments will explore the upper atmosphere. They will also record interactions with the sun and solar wind. These data will give insight into the history of Mars's climate and could explain why Mars lost most of its atmosphere. Together with other missions, MAVEN hopes to determine whether life could once have been present on Mars.

from reaching solar panels. The terrain on Mars is rocky and uneven, and there is no roadside assistance if a rover gets stuck.

Fortunately, *Curiosity* benefited from the lessons learned during the missions before it. *Curiosity* copied many features of previous successful rovers. Like NASA's earlier rovers *Spirit* and *Opportunity*, it has six wheels. A special suspension system enables these vehicles to keep all six wheels on the ground at once, even on uneven terrain. The front and rear wheels can be independently steered.

Engineer Jaime Waydo led the team that designed and built the *Curiosity* mobility system. This includes the wheels, suspension, and other parts that allow the rover to land and then roll over the Martian terrain. They needed a system that was as light as possible yet strong enough to handle the heavy load.

The mobility team used a model rover to test the mechanisms that would unlock the wheels during landing. Waydo remembered how she felt during the testing:

> *My hands are sweating, and my throat is getting dry, and I'm looking at it going, "Oh, my goodness. Oh, my goodness." And then, they let it go, and she hit, and it was so hard. . . . That tangible, visceral, "What does landing look like?" is much different on a computer simulation than, than the first time you see it for real.*[4]

Curiosity is bigger than previous Mars rovers, approximately twice as long as *Spirit* and *Opportunity*. *Curiosity* is also five times as heavy as its earlier cousins. This required a redesign of the rover's wheels. The team took inspiration from the most common vehicle on Earth: bicycles. Waydo said, "We talked to a bicycle company that makes titanium bikes, and they helped us build the suspension tubes. We ended up taking a bicycle wheel and making it as strong as possible and taking that to the extreme and making it, basically, a Martian bicycle wheel."[5]

With its large wheels, *Curiosity* can roll over obstacles up to 25 inches (64 cm) high.[6] Sand had been a problem for previous Mars rovers, but the wide wheels on *Curiosity* had no trouble when tested on sand dunes.

Curiosity's large size meant a wheel failure could result in serious damage. The mobility system was subjected to intensive testing on Earth.

GETTING AROUND

Keeping a rover running is another challenge. It needs a source of power that will last the full duration of the planned mission or even longer. NASA's earlier rovers depended on solar power. This meant they could not work at night and had to hibernate in winter. *Curiosity* instead uses a radioisotope generator (RTG). As the radioactive element plutonium-238 decays inside the RTG, it produces heat that can be converted into electricity. The RTG provides enough power to operate the rover's wheels, computers, radio, and instruments. In addition, the RTG's heat warms up fluids that help keep systems at a healthy temperature. Radioisotope power systems last longer than solar and do not require sunlight. *Curiosity*'s RTG is expected to provide power for at least 14 years.[7]

Curiosity is able to travel farther than previous rovers, but controlling a car on Mars is not a simple matter. Commands travel by radio waves at the speed of light. The time of this journey depends on how far Mars is from Earth and can take up to 24 minutes.[8] With so much delay, the rover could crash or flip over before the human driver on Earth even knew an obstacle was coming.

For this reason, controlling a rover from Earth is a slow, cautious process. Typically, the mission team plans out which areas to explore. A camera mounted on the rover helps the team identify targets and find

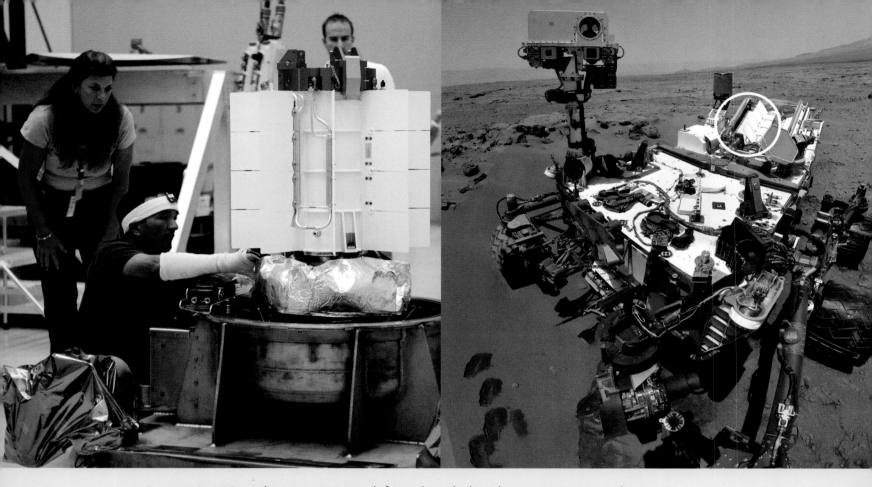

Curiosity's RTG under construction, *left,* and circled at the rover's rear, *right*

good driving routes. A rover driver on Earth views the target site on a computer screen through virtual-reality goggles and sends commands to the rover.

Curiosity can also navigate by itself, intelligently deciding when it needs to avoid obstacles. Engineers adapted software that had been used on *Spirit* and *Opportunity* for the larger and more complex *Curiosity*. The rover takes side-by-side pairs of images, giving it a sense of depth perception. Its computer analyzes the images to map any rough terrain. It considers the paths it could take and chooses the best one.

The automatic navigation allows *Curiosity* to travel in areas that would otherwise be unsafe. For example, one mission took *Curiosity* across a depression with unknown surface details. Rover driver John Wright said, "We could see the area before the dip, and we told the rover where to drive on that part. We could see the ground on the other side, where we designated a point for the rover to end the drive, but *Curiosity* figured out for herself how to drive the uncharted part in between."[9]

CURIOSITY AT WORK

In many ways, *Curiosity* fared better than its engineers dared hope. It was originally scheduled for a two-year mission, but that will be extended as long as the rover continues to function. *Curiosity*'s power source could sustain the rover for many years. The success of *Curiosity*, and the lessons engineers learn from it, will help future missions. NASA wants to launch another unmanned rover, based heavily on *Curiosity*. This new rover will scoop up a sample of Martian rock and soil. Then, another spacecraft will arrive to carry the sample back to Earth.

The data and photographs *Curiosity* collected will keep scientists busy for years to come.

MORE POWER

Curiosity benefited from general technological advances as well as previous mission results. Computers are much more powerful than they were a decade ago. The computers on *Curiosity* have about eight times the memory of the ones on *Spirit* and *Opportunity*.[11] Still, the computing power on *Curiosity* is much less than you would find in a modern home computer. Though *Curiosity* launched in 2011, the computer it uses was originally released in 2001. Computers used in spacecraft are usually older versions that have proven themselves highly reliable. They also must be specially designed to resist heat, cold, and radiation.

Colleen Hartman, a senior NASA manager, said before *Curiosity*'s launch, "It's an order of magnitude more capable than anything we have ever launched to any planet in the solar system. It will go longer, it will discover more than we can possibly imagine."[10] So far, her prediction has proven correct.

A ROBOT SURGEON

The word *robot* may bring to mind the metallic humanoid figures of science-fiction movies. However, robots are simply computer-controlled machines that can carry out complex tasks. Many types exist today in a variety of shapes and sizes. While they seldom look human, they do some of the jobs humans have done in the past, from carrying heavy loads to working on assembly lines. Because robots are machines, mechanical engineers are often involved in their design and development.

Building a robot that can mimic human motions is a tremendous challenge. Human hands are remarkable tools. Guided by memory and

Once a science-fiction dream, surgery-performing robots are now being introduced to hospitals all around the world.

experience, they can quickly complete a task such as tying a ribbon into a bow. While this may not look difficult, it requires the fingers to work with dexterity and precision through a series of small, complex motions. A human is also aided by sensory feedback. In this case, that means the ability to see what is happening and feel when fingers are touching each other or the ribbon.

For a robot to duplicate this process, it must match these abilities. If the robot hands do not have joints, they will not be flexible enough. Without sensors, the robot cannot see the ribbon or feel it moving. It would be like trying to tie a bow while blindfolded and wearing thick gloves.

Despite the design challenges, robots have improved greatly in the last century. Now they can replicate many human tasks. Robots have replaced humans in some jobs, such as some types of factory work. In other cases, they work alongside people to complete tasks more efficiently or accurately.

A ROBOT DOCTOR

The da Vinci Surgical System is a robot that helps doctors perform surgery. The surgeon stays in control, but the robot makes the surgeon's job easier. To the surgeon, the system works rather like a video game.

The surgeon sits at a console and views three-dimensional (3-D) images from inside the patient's body. The patient lies nearby on an operating table, surrounded by three or four robotic arms. The surgeon moves her or his hands and wrists to control the robot's action. The computer system

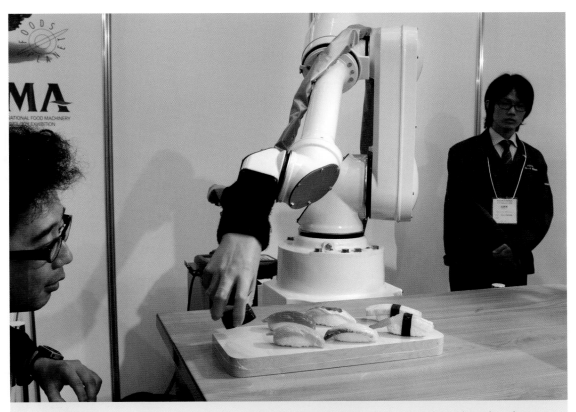

The last decade has seen impressive advances in robotic hand technology.

BOTS LIKE US

From an engineering point of view, the human body is a system much like a robot. When a human makes a decision to move, the brain conveys the decision to the muscles. While the muscles move, the nervous system provides feedback from the senses to help the person avoid running into things. Movement involves the senses, muscles, brain, and nervous system working together.

When a robot receives instructions to move, the command must be conveyed to its motors. The motors control movement, while sensors might detect obstacles through light, sound, or touch. A computer, sensors, wires, and motors work together when the robot moves. Robotics engineers are researching the human body and trying to replicate the way it functions. Understanding the human body helps engineers develop better robots. At the same time, the principles used in robotics are useful for understanding the human body.

translates the surgeon's movements on the controls into the movement of the robotic arms.

This system offers several advantages to a surgeon working directly on a patient. The enlarged 3-D images help the surgeon see better. The multiple robot arms can hold several different tools while bending and rotating more than a human wrist can. The system translates the surgeon's movements into smaller, more precise movements on tiny instruments.

This allows the surgeon to overcome the limits of the human hand while still keeping his or her experienced mind in control.

The makers of the da Vinci system, Intuitive Surgical, claim this robot-assisted surgery has many benefits. Because the surgical incisions are smaller, the patient may lose less blood and have smaller scars. Patients may recover faster with a shorter hospital stay, which saves money.

Despite all the advantages, robotic surgery systems are not perfect. They are not delicate enough for some types of surgery on small children. The bulky equipment limits the operating room staff's access to the patient. At approximately $1 million, plus the cost of yearly maintenance and physician training, the equipment is also too expensive for many hospitals.[1] These challenges offer opportunities for mechanical engineers. The future may see smaller, cheaper designs with even better features.

TYPES OF SURGERY

Robotic surgery has three subcategories. In the first, a supervisory-control system, the surgeon inputs a computer program in advance to control the robot. The robot then executes the procedure alone. In a telesurgical system, also known as remote surgery, the surgeon manipulates the robotic arms during the procedure. The surgeon may operate from a remote location. The da Vinci Surgical System falls in this category. Finally, in a shared-control system, the surgeon and robot work together. The surgeon carries out the procedure, but the robot offers help steadying the instruments.

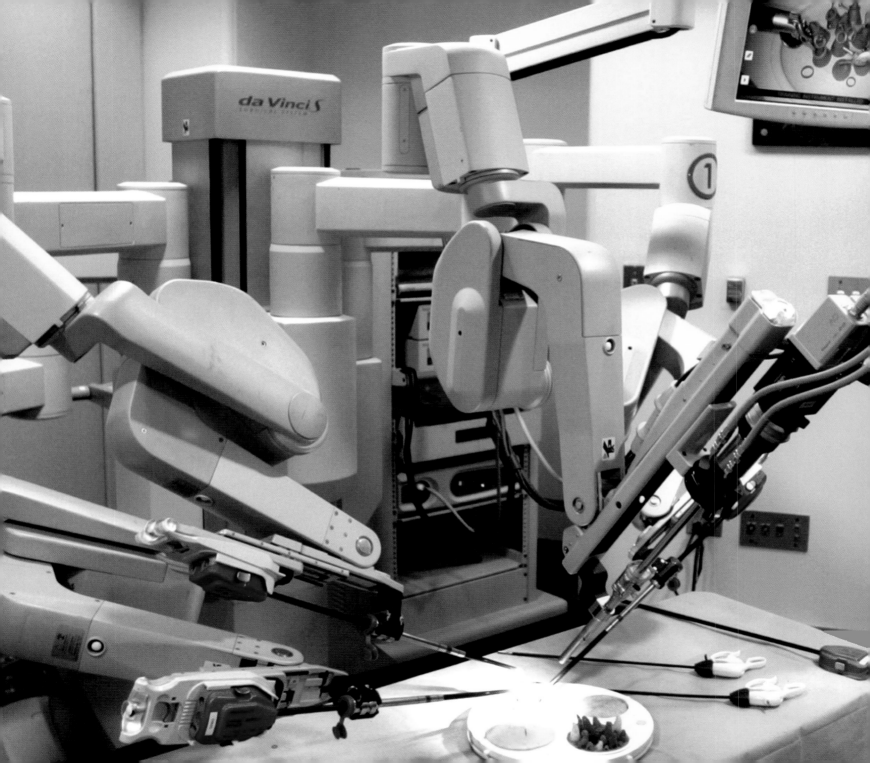

The da Vinci Surgical System is a large
and very expensive piece of equipment.

CHALLENGES ALONG THE WAY

Similar to the Mars rovers, the da Vinci Surgical System involved the work
of many people over many years. It got its start in the late 1980s with
government funding. The Defense Advanced Research Projects Agency
(DARPA), a branch of the US Department of Defense, supports research
that might benefit the military. DARPA wanted a robotic system that
would enable surgeons to operate from a remote location. This would
allow surgeons to treat soldiers injured in battle by using robots installed
in armored vehicles. DARPA provided funding to several US research
centers to pursue these goals. Without this funding, the advances in
surgical technology might never have happened.

One of the research centers that received funding, the Stanford
Research Institute, developed a robotic surgery system. However, the
surgeon had to remain fairly close to the patient, limiting the system's
use on the battlefield. Frederic Moll, a medical equipment specialist, saw
how the system could be used outside of the military. "The public has no
idea of the extent of difference between top surgeons and bad ones,"
Moll said in an interview. He thought robotic surgery could even out these
differences. "Robots are good at going where they are supposed to,
remembering where they are, and stopping when required."[2]

Moll found investors, negotiated for use of the technology, and founded Intuitive Surgical to bring the product to market. The new company added to the Stanford technology with its own advances and those from other research groups. Engineers with specialties in robots, including Kenneth Salisbury from the Massachusetts Institute of Technology, were hired to help develop the robotic surgery system. The first prototype of the da Vinci Surgical System was used in animal trials in 1996. Human trials began in 1997 using a second prototype.

A big challenge for getting any medical device to the market is government approval. The US Food and Drug Administration (FDA) is a government agency responsible for protecting the public's health. The FDA regulates food, dietary supplements, human and veterinary drugs, cosmetics, and more. A branch of the FDA regulates companies that design and manufacture medical devices. A company must show that a new device is safe and effective before it can sell the product. FDA approval can take many years. Another robotic surgery system, the RoboDoc, was introduced in 1992. It entered use in Europe but did not receive FDA clearance for US use until 2008.

Before a medical device is approved, a company may get permission to use it in clinical studies. This allows the company to collect data on safety and effectiveness. Intuitive Surgical tested the da Vinci system on

MILITARY ADVANCES

DARPA was founded in 1958 to do research that would help protect US security. Today the group works on highly experimental technology intended to improve US military and defense systems. This includes battlefield tools such as armored vehicles, drones, and equipment to jam communications. Much of the technology is classified for national security reasons. However, some technologies make it to the public. For example, DARPA helped develop the groundwork for the Internet in the 1960s and 1970s.

Today, the military uses robots in many ways. Some robots perform bomb disposal and other dangerous missions. Others simply carry heavy loads. Some use sensors to get information about the surrounding area. They can look inside buildings or around corners.

113 patients and compared the results with 132 patients who received standard surgery.[3] The robotic system was shown to be comparable in safety and effectiveness. If traditional surgery had been better, the robotic system could not have been released without further improvements and testing. In 1999, the da Vinci Surgical System became the first assisting surgical robot to receive FDA approval.

Even after a medical device is approved, additional clinical studies are needed if the device is modified or is to be used for a new purpose. The da Vinci system was originally approved for use in only a few procedures, such as gallbladder surgery. Other uses required additional FDA approval. In July 2000, the da Vinci Surgical System received FDA approval for laparoscopic surgery. This is a type of surgery involving a small incision and a tiny camera, making it a natural fit for a robotic surgical system.

The da Vinci Surgical System seemed poised to become an important part of operating rooms everywhere. However, with complicated technology, getting a product to market is not the end of the process. The job of mechanical engineers is not over when the first version of a product is released. Intuitive Surgical would face many difficulties in the following years as their product entered widespread use.

WHY "DA VINCI"?

The da Vinci Surgical System was named after inventor, painter, and philosopher Leonardo da Vinci. He helped advance the study of human anatomy with his detailed anatomical drawings based on autopsies. He was also fascinated by mechanics and automation. He developed moving mannequins, including a mechanical knight. He even drew designs for a robot around the year 1495.

Kenneth Salisbury received his PhD in mechanical engineering from Stanford University. He then worked as a scientist at the Massachusetts Institute of Technology (MIT), leading projects involving surgical robots and robot hands.

One of his specialty areas is haptics, the sense of touch that is used to perceive or manipulate an object. In robotics, haptics give users the feeling that they are touching an actual object, when in reality they are using a touch screen, joystick, or other device. Salisbury and fellow professor Thomas Massie developed the PHANTOM haptic interface at MIT. The user holds a stylus or wears a fingertip thimble. The device tracks the motion of the user's finger while providing sensitive feedback. This can help train surgeons in simulated procedures.

In 1997, Salisbury joined Intuitive Surgical as an adviser. Now a professor in the computer science and surgery departments at Stanford University, he focuses on medical robotics. He is especially interested in how humans and machines interact.

The robotic hands Salisbury developed broke new ground in control and sensitivity.

TROUBLESHOOTING DA VINCI

Making a robot that can perform as well as a human surgeon is an incredibly complex task. Because patients' lives are at risk, any flaws in the device can have serious or even fatal consequences. All surgery carries risks, but when a death is the result of equipment failure, the company that made the product is typically blamed.

Engineers at Intuitive Surgical included several safety mechanisms in the da Vinci system. A battery backup allows the system to continue running if the power goes out. If the surgeon is not present in the control console, the system will lock and remain motionless. Each of the

The engineers and doctors of Intuitive Surgical faced challenges even after their product's release.

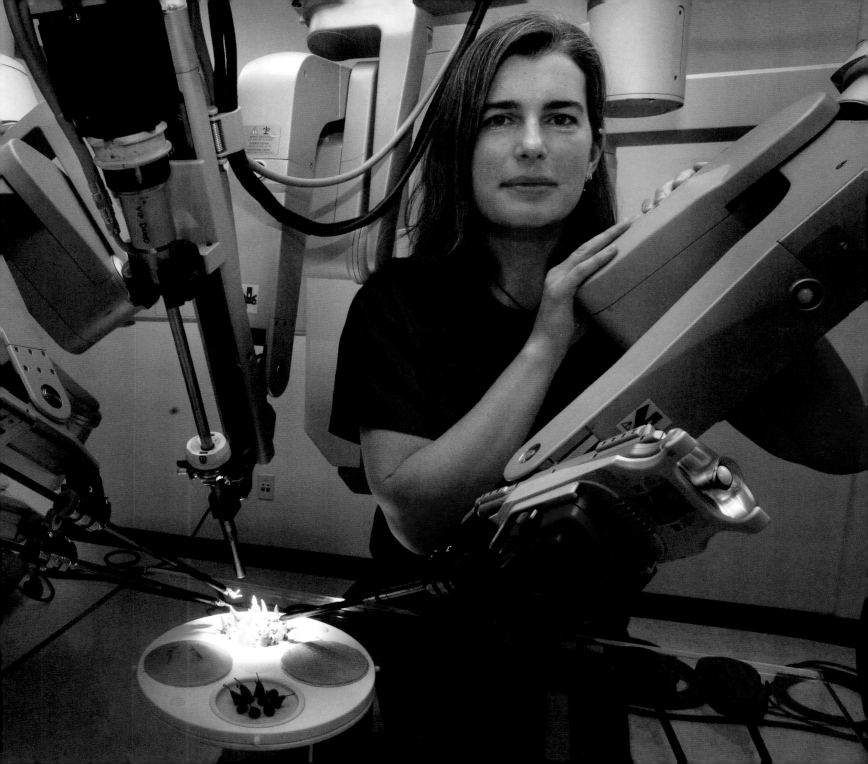

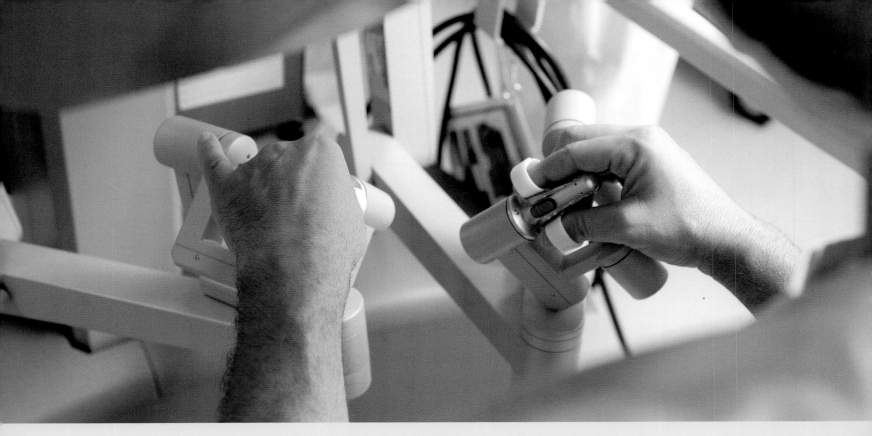

Doctors use hand controls to operate the da Vinci robotic surgery system.

robot's tools is designed to tell the operator when it should be replaced, preventing surgeons from using worn-out parts.

Despite these safety measures, unexpected problems cropped up. In 2013, Intuitive Surgical issued an urgent notice about a problem with the system. One of the instruments that can be used on the system's robotic arms is a pair of curved scissors. Some of the scissors had developed microscopic cracks. These tiny cracks were not visible to the naked eye, but they could result in electric burns to patients. Intuitive Surgical provided replacement scissors within a few weeks of announcing the problem.

Technical problems such as these often lead to legal problems. In May 2013, Intuitive Surgical was the defendant in several product liability lawsuits. The various plaintiffs claimed equipment defects or inadequate surgeon training led to injuries or deaths. Intuitive Surgical claimed it had a strong defense against these charges. Still, lawsuits cost time and money, and they can hurt a company's reputation.

Not all the lawsuits Intuitive Surgical faced came from patients or their heirs. Another company, Computer Motion, was developing robotic surgery systems at the same time as Intuitive Surgical. These competitors entered a fierce legal battle. Computer Motion filed a lawsuit against Intuitive Surgical for nine patent infringements. Intuitive Surgical responded by filing three lawsuits against Computer Motion. It also teamed with the International Business Machines Corporation (IBM) to sue Computer Motion for infringing on its voice-recognition technology. Computer Motion lost this case, which meant it could no longer sell its devices without a license from Intuitive Surgical.

In 2003, the two companies merged. Intuitive Surgical bought Computer Motion and continued to market its products but fired approximately 90 percent of its employees.[1] Most mechanical engineers would hope to avoid legal disputes such as these in their careers. Still, these conflicts provide work for people with a background in both mechanical engineering and law.

THE IMPORTANCE OF TESTING

New technology can be exciting, both for the creator and for users. However, new technology is not always an improvement on the past. To understand whether a new product really offers advantages, experts need to collect and analyze data.

For the da Vinci system, thousands of mishaps were reported to the FDA between January 2000 and August 2012. In most cases, the patient was not harmed, but the reports included 174 injuries and 71 deaths related to da Vinci surgery. However, more than a million procedures had been performed.[2] Knowing only those numbers alone, it is impossible to say whether da Vinci surgery is unusually safe or unsafe. Accurate numbers must be collected for all surgical methods for comparison. Yet experts believe surgery complications are vastly underreported, making this comparison difficult.

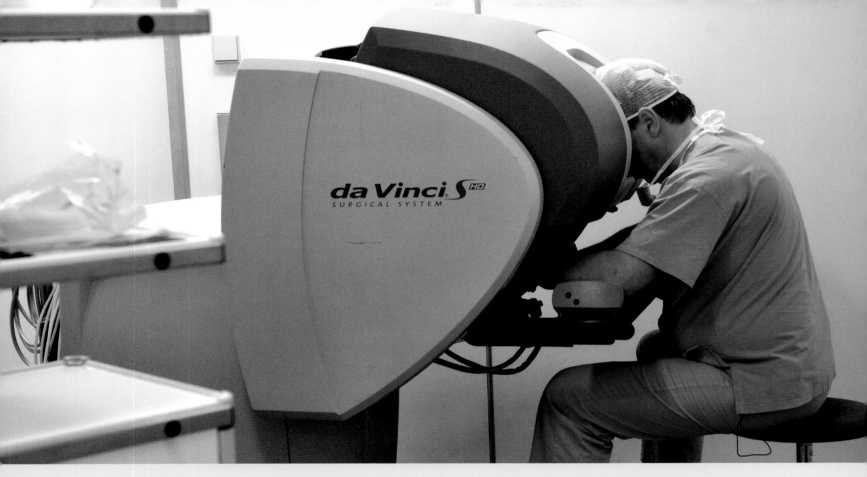

Surgeons sit at a large control console when using the da Vinci system.

Facilities are required to report problems to the FDA. Yet doctors and hospitals may fail to do so, either because they do not want to be blamed for injuries or to avoid the hassles of paperwork. According to experts, only a small number of surgical complications are reported to the FDA. This makes it impossible to determine the true failure rates for different types of equipment. According to Martin A. Makary of Johns Hopkins University, "This whole issue is symbolic of a larger problem in American health care, which is the lack of proper evaluation of what we do. We adopt expensive new technologies, but we don't even know what we're getting for our money—if it's of good value or harmful."[3]

Mechanical engineers can help prevent injuries and lawsuits by doing thorough testing before releasing a product. After brainstorming and evaluating ideas, an engineering team begins building prototypes. This helps determine whether ideas that look good on paper will work in reality. A prototype should be a fully functional model. This allows the engineers to test the product for usability and determine when and how it could fail. If the prototype does not meet the design requirements, the process starts over. Engineers redesign, rebuild, and retest.

This may happen several times in the quest for a successful prototype. Once the team is satisfied with the prototype, it can build the actual product. Tests continue in an effort to catch lingering design problems and manufacturing defects.

WORKING FOR THE FUTURE

It can take years for a company to develop a product, get necessary FDA approvals, handle legal challenges, manufacture the item, and release it for sale. Even then, most products are not truly finished once they reach the market. There are always options for upgrades or improved versions. The da Vinci System has had several upgrades over the years. The first major upgrade offered an additional instrument arm. A later model offered high-definition vision for the first time, plus a simplified set up. The da Vinci Si System, released in 2009, allowed two surgeons to work together on separate consoles.

STUCK AT PROTOTYPE

Not all prototypes will lead to a finished product. In the late 1990s, a system similar to the da Vinci Surgical System was developed in Germany. This system, known as ARTEMIS, was the first to introduce certain features, including 3-D visualization. A prototype was built, but the device never made it to market. The prototype was used to demonstrate the system. It was declared feasible, though additional technical development was needed. A prototype can be a valuable part of the design process, even if that particular device does not reach the market.

Future advances will likely attempt to fix some of the problems discovered so far and also offer more benefits. Many surgeons would like more sensory feedback to replicate the feel of hands-on surgery. Updates may also make robotic surgery suitable for more people in more situations. Finally, medical robots may be able to help prepare the patient for surgery, reducing the number of medical staff needed in the room.

One of the dreams for the future of robotic surgery is long-distance telesurgery. This would allow a doctor to perform surgery while miles away from the patient. An expert surgeon could perform surgery on someone across the country or around the world. So far, long-distance telesurgery has been difficult to perfect. The robotic system reacts instantly to the doctor's hand movements only if the doctor is close to the patient. This time delay over long distance could be dangerous for patients. Some long-distance tests of telesurgery have been conducted. They showed the procedure is feasible, though it is not yet widely accepted. If engineers improve the technology, then the original goal of surgeons remotely operating on the battlefield could be met.

How much of surgery will be taken over by robots? Building a product, even if it is a futuristic robotic surgeon, does not necessarily mean people will want to use it. Still, "If you are looking at the future, it's hard to envision a hospital not offering robotics," said Robert Glenning of the

Hackensack University Medical Center.[4] The good news for mechanical engineers is that the issues and problems facing robotic surgery represent an array of opportunities.

In September 2001, a surgeon in New York City operated on a patient in France in an early demonstration of telesurgery.

CHAPTER 7

POWER FROM THE AIR

Mechanical engineers are at the forefront of solving many of the world's technical problems. Addressing environmental issues, including climate change, is high on the list of these challenges. John Holdren, science and technology adviser to President Barack Obama, suggested people have three choices when it comes to climate change: mitigation, adaptation, or suffering. "We're going to do some of each. The question is what the mix is going to be. The more mitigation we do, the less adaptation will be required and the less suffering there will be."[1]

The engineering problem of improving alternative energy sources has become a politically significant issue.

Many modern buildings feature
environmentally friendly features such
as solar panels and rooftop parks.

Scientists, engineers, and others are responding to the challenge with innovative technology. Mechanical engineers can help in many ways. For example, they can design engines that are more efficient or less polluting than current versions. They can produce technology to help factories and power plants reduce air pollution. They can help limit climate change by developing renewable energy.

The environmental impact of mechanical engineering may be most obvious when it comes to energy. Energy is needed for businesses, homes, factories, and cars. The world demand for energy is expected to increase 43 percent by 2035.[2] Most of our energy today comes from fossil fuels, and this is likely to continue for decades to come. Yet fossil fuels are highly polluting and contribute to global climate change.

Alternative energy sources are important for reducing pollution and stemming future climate change. They are also important because traditional fossil fuel resources are limited. Among the most promising alternative energy sources are water, sunlight, and wind. Solar energy is most effective in sunny regions. Hydroelectric dams make sense only where large amounts of water flow. Wind turbines are most useful in windy areas. Because they are suitable for different areas, each of

CENTURIES OF WIND POWER

Harnessing the wind is not a new concept. A Persian windmill dating to the 600s is the earliest-known attempt to use wind power. Two types of windmills were developed in Europe in the 1200s. These windmills were used primarily to pump water or grind grain.

The wind turbine is a form of windmill. More than 18,000 wind turbines operate in the United States.[3] Wind energy does not yet provide a large portion of US power, but it is growing in popularity every year. Wind power capacity nearly doubled between 2011 and 2012. The 2012 capacity was 22 times what it was in the year 2000.[4] Western and midwestern states use the most wind power. Most western states have passed laws requiring energy companies to provide some of their energy from renewable sources.

US Energy Secretary Ernest Moniz said, "As the fastest growing source of power in the United States, wind is paving the way to a cleaner, more sustainable future that protects our air and water and provides affordable, clean renewable energy to more and more Americans."[5]

these forms of alternative energy has a place in the future. Mechanical engineers will help improve the technologies to make them cheaper and more efficient.

WIND POWER

People have harnessed the power of the wind for centuries. Today's wind turbines usually have spinning blades atop a narrow tower. These towers may be 300 feet (91 m) tall or more.[6] Height is important because wind is faster and less turbulent higher above ground. The spinning blades capture the natural kinetic energy of the wind. This is then converted into electric energy.

Wind helps power more than 15 million homes in the United States, or more than 10 percent of the nation's homes.[7] Worldwide, wind energy has been the fastest growing energy technology for a decade. Some experts predict wind power will contribute 12 to 14 percent of the European Union's electricity demand by 2020.[8] A single small turbine might power one home, business, or farm. When wind power is used in the utility industry, many large turbines are connected to the power grid. They can provide power to hundreds or thousands of homes.

Larger wind turbines produce more energy than smaller ones. The largest wind turbine in the world is the E-126, made by Enercon. This German corporation was established in 1984 by Aloys Wobben. Each E-126 tower rises more than 440 feet (134 m) high. With the spinning blades, the entire installation reaches approximately 650 feet (198 m) into the air. A single E-126 turbine produces enough energy to power thousands of homes.[9]

LARGE OR SMALL?

In recent years, technical innovations have improved wind turbines. They can now be larger, with longer, lighter blades. This has improved power output and allowed wind turbines to be used in less windy areas. Still, most wind turbines installed in the United States are much smaller than the E-126. They are useful for powering small communities. Even when wind cannot provide enough power for an entire city, adding several small wind power plants helps improve the efficiency and reliability of the power grid.

A larger turbine has the advantage of producing more power than smaller ones, but installing such a big piece of machinery is challenging. Each E-126 rotor blade is 193 feet (59 m) long. To make transportation easier, the E-126 blades come in two pieces. A 115-foot (35 m) outer section is bolted onto a 79-foot (24 m) inner section. These and other large pieces must be transported from the manufacturing site to the installation site. Simply moving the pieces for a single E-126 is an engineering marvel in itself. The process can take up to 100 trips with special heavy-duty trucks. Joining the two blade sections takes three workers a day and a half per blade.[10]

During the installation of an E-126 turbine, heavy pieces must be lifted high into the air. Workers at a wind farm in Belgium used a special giant crane, the largest of its type in the world, designed and built especially to meet the needs of the E-126. Previous installations required three smaller cranes. The larger crane added its own complications. It had to be dismantled in order to move even a short distance. Once it was reassembled, it had to be inspected. The entire process took up to three weeks for each move.

BUILDING TO LAST

An important part of any design is making sure the product is sturdy and safe. This means choosing the best materials. Every material is affected by tension and compression, two forces that mechanical engineers must always keep in mind. Tension is any force that pulls materials apart. Compression is any force that squeezes materials together. These forces affect the building of structures whether they are small or large. One material, such as rope, may withstand tension when pulled but bend when compressed. Another material, such as marshmallow, may compress easily but fall apart when under tension.

A material may even experience compression and tension at the same time. For example, when a beam is supported on two pillars, it may sag in the middle. The bottom of the beam is under tension, lengthening as it stretches. The top of the beam is under compression, shortening as it squeezes together. If a weight is placed on top of the beam, it increases those stresses. If the forces are strong enough, the beam may break.

Mechanical engineers must choose the right materials for their products in order to withstand tension and compression. This is especially challenging with large, outdoor structures, such as buildings, bridges, and wind turbines. They must withstand not just everyday conditions, but also unusual ones, such as snow, ice, and high winds. In some areas, structures may even need to withstand earthquakes. A large structure cannot be tested in the lab, so engineers use mathematical models to predict how a structure will react to different loads.

When it comes to choosing the right materials for a structure, there is seldom a single, easy answer. Many factors affect the final decision, including strength, weight, stiffness, durability, cost, and more.

A WEIGHTY PROBLEM

Many parts of the E-126 are made from aluminum. Aluminum is relatively light, but because some pieces of the E-126 are so large, they weigh hundreds of tons. The turbine needs a sturdy piece of ground to support the weight. If the soil is not stable enough, the turbine could collapse.

Enercon faced unsuitable soil when installing turbines at the Belgian wind farm. Engineers had to determine a way to build a steady base for the huge structure. The company dug a circular hole 130 feet (40 m)

E-126 turbines were constructed in Sweden in
2010 as part of a wind farm that is planned
to include more than 1,000 turbines.

across and 16 feet (5 m) deep. Then it drilled approximately 200 columns throughout the hole.[11] The columns were filled with special gravel, which was compressed tightly. The entire hole was then covered with a thick, level layer of more gravel reinforced by special fabric. A thin concrete layer went over everything. This process helped distribute the load of the turbine over a larger area.

That was not the only problem to crop up during the installation in Belgium. An underground fuel line crossed fairly close to two turbines. Authorities required the fuel line be covered by a concrete lining for 1.25 miles (2 km). This would protect it in case a rotor blade fell or was thrown from the turbine. Safety guidelines try to prevent even the most unlikely danger.

When a technology is new, engineers may have to adapt to many unexpected challenges. In an interview during the installation process, a representative of the wind farm development company said, "In general, this project represents a major almost daily challenge to all parties involved."[12]

CHAPTER 8

KEEPING THE LIGHTS ON

Unfortunately, even technology that benefits the environment may have negative environmental effects. To understand these effects, scientists use computer models and study the technology in action.

Birds and bats can be killed by colliding with wind turbines. However, research has helped reduce the number of deaths. For example, wildlife biologists found that bats are most active when wind speeds are low. Therefore, bat deaths can be reduced by keeping wind turbines

Though turbines kill birds, studies show pollution from fossil fuel power plants is much more deadly to birds.

FUNDING CLEAN ENERGY

The growth of clean energy depends partly on the government. President Obama's administration provided tax credits for clean energy development and supported other clean energy policies. Because elections frequently change government policy, support for clean energy can also change. When elections are upcoming, projects may be put on hold until the future is clear.

Many of the world's governments subsidize the fossil fuel industry, even though it is a major cause of pollution. In 2012, fossil fuels received $544 billion in government subsidies. Renewable energy received less than 20 percent of that, totaling $101 billion. Experts expect subsidies for renewable energy to more than double in the next 20 years.[1] However, without reform, fossil fuels will still receive much more government support.

motionless when winds are slow. It is also important to find the right site for a wind farm in order to reduce the impact on wildlife habitats.

Offshore wind farms may be installed on submerged sandbanks. Construction could impact the marine mammals and seabirds living in those areas. Some studies show offshore wind farms are not a great danger to birds and may even help fish populations by acting as artificial reefs. Every site is different, though, and must be properly researched and monitored.

Engineers must also consider how their designs will affect people. Some people dislike the appearance of wind farms. Wind turbines produce little pollution, but people living near wind farms have complained about the sound and vibration. While studies have shown these issues do not affect public health, unhappy communities threaten the expansion of wind farms. Any large project may require open discussions with the community to head off problems. In most cases, properly placing the wind farm can reduce complaints about the noise and appearance. Other steps, such as planting trees to separate residential areas from wind farms, can also help.

THE WOUNDS OF TIME

Engineers have many factors to consider when planning any project. This is especially true for a large project that affects the public, such as a wind farm. Part of the challenge is simply preparing for the damage caused by time. Outdoor structures such as wind turbines break down over time due to weathering. This can involve disintegration, including physical breakdown such as cracks. It can also involve decomposition, which is chemical breakdown. Acids produced by living things or by pollution cause decomposition. Structures have been deteriorating more quickly in recent decades because of pollution.

Disintegration and decomposition can combine to speed up weathering. For example, a crack in a wall can allow chemical weathering to reach inside the wall. The resulting decomposition may weaken the material, increasing the likelihood of more cracks. Engineers must consider these aspects of weathering when working on outdoor structures. Sturdier materials may cost more up front but save money by lasting longer. For some uses, extremely high quality is not needed and therefore would be a waste of money.

Even seemingly simple materials, such as concrete, can vary dramatically in makeup. Concrete is a mixture of water, cement, rock, and sand. The water and cement form a paste, which coats the gravel and sand. As the paste hardens, it gains strength. This means concrete is easily shaped when freshly mixed, but it is strong and long lasting when hard. The type and size of the rock and sand are chosen based on the thickness and purpose of the concrete. Even the type of water makes a difference. Water that contains many impurities may affect the concrete's strength and durability. Concrete's strength depends on the type and amount of each material, the mixing method, and how the solution was poured. In general, concrete with less water and more cement will be stronger.

However, it is harder to mix and form. Other materials, such as steel bars, can be used to reinforce concrete and make it stronger.

E-126 wind turbines use concrete for many components, including foundations, walls, and towers. Enercon developed its own process for making concrete towers. Carts running on rails overhead continually add liquid concrete to a reservoir. This reservoir distributes the material into cone-shaped molds. Most of this production is automated, using robots rather than human workers. By making its own concrete, Enercon controls the quality.

STAYING HEALTHY

No matter how well built a structure is, it can suffer damage over time. Wind turbines are especially complex because the force and direction of the wind constantly changes. Understanding how the wind's behavior affects the turbine is important for protecting it from the stress of high winds.

Wind turbines must be constantly monitored for signs of damage. Structural health monitoring (SHM) is an important engineering process for many large structures. SHM is intended to detect unusual behaviors and identify the source of the problem. It may even trigger safety responses. This monitoring is done through a network of sensors placed throughout the structure.

Maintaining enormous wind turbines can be a dangerous job.

Inspecting and servicing a huge wind turbine is difficult. SHM can help identify trouble spots remotely. This improves safety and can save money, since parts can be repaired before they fail.

For a moving structure such as a wind turbine, SHM can also provide feedback on performance. With sensor feedback, a wind turbine's blades may be controlled individually. Wind speed and gust strength can vary from the top of a wind turbine to the bottom. Controlling the blades separately helps balance the forces, preventing stress. This level of control means turbines can use larger blades to capture more energy. Monitoring performance also makes it possible to run the windmill efficiently during times of low wind.

ALWAYS ROOM FOR ADVANCEMENT

For wind power to meet its maximum potential, wind turbines must keep improving. Engineers find ideas for improvements in many places. One company is designing turbine blades inspired by humpback whale fins. This came about almost by accident. Biologist Frank E. Fish saw a sculpture of a humpback whale and thought, "The sculptor put the bumps on the wrong side of the flipper."[2] The sculpture was actually accurate. It went against what Fish knew of movement through fluids. Engineers

HOLDING ON TO WIND POWER

One of the major criticisms of wind energy is that it works only when the wind is blowing. What's more, during times of heavy wind, power may be lost because it cannot all be stored. In 2013, General Electric introduced a wind turbine and power management system, the GE Brilliant 1.6-100. It incorporates short-term battery storage so energy can be saved until it is needed. This allows the turbine to supply power more evenly.

The new power management system uses customized software to maximize efficiency. It instantly adjusts to factors such as speed, torque, and other properties of the air and the turbine. This improved efficiency is expected to boost power output by up to 5 percent. That is enough to power approximately 18 additional homes per turbine.[4] The software also analyzes performance. Engineers can use this data to further improve the technology.

had believed the leading edge of finlike structures had to be smooth to work properly.

Fish and other scientists tested designs based on the whale fin to understand the science. It turned out a blade with a bumpy leading edge can be used at a steeper angle. A steeper angle provides more power, but too steep an angle would normally create drag and stall the motor. Adding the bumps lets blades work at a steeper angle without stalling.

Carefully shaping turbine blades is key in maximizing their efficiency.

This new design could allow wind farms to increase electric production by 20 percent.[3]

Wind power must also be used in more areas if it is to become a major source of energy. Many coastal countries have installed wind farms offshore. It is more expensive to develop offshore wind farms, but they can produce more power, because offshore wind is stronger and steadier. Wind blowing over land loses some of its strength as mountains and valleys disrupt it.

The E-126 was initially used exclusively on land. In 2013, Enercon made plans to install a prototype version at a testing site off the coast of France. This would test the turbine in higher-speed coastal winds. So far, the E-126 seems well suited to offshore use.

OFFSHORE POWER POTENTIAL

The United States has almost 100,000 miles (161,000 km) of coastline, and 39 percent of the nation's population lives near the coast.[5] This would seem to make offshore wind farms an ideal energy source. However, offshore wind energy has been slow to take hold in the United States. Installing offshore wind farms is approximately twice as expensive as similar projects on land. Communities may also express concern about everything from the impact on wildlife to ruining the view.

CHAPTER 9

THE FUTURE OF ENGINEERING

Mechanical engineers build products that improve the quality of life. These range from better transportation methods to entertainment systems to toys. Many devices make work easier and leisure time more fun. Others help save lives. Engineering even helps scientists explore the universe, from the deepest oceans to outer space. These means of expanding human knowledge feed our curiosity and may contribute to a better tomorrow.

The future holds many challenges that engineering can help solve. The world's population is growing quickly, putting a strain on resources.

Mechanical engineers work to push the boundaries of human knowledge and achievement.

WOMEN AT WORK

Women have traditionally made up a very small percentage of mechanical engineers. Studies have shown that women engineering students perform as well as men, but only approximately 20 percent of engineering degrees go to women.[1] Still, women who go into engineering often find satisfying careers. Some appreciate being able to combine skills and areas of interest, such as using technical skills to help people and the environment.

Women are also well represented at NASA. The Jet Propulsion Laboratory team in charge of the *Curiosity* rover's launch included several women. Erisa Hines, attitude control system engineer, said in an interview, "The fact that I get to work on things I think are really exciting and challenging is a big reward. Flying a spacecraft to Mars is such a unique thing to do."[2]

Improving the quality of life for everyone must be balanced with protecting Earth itself. The population currently consumes resources at a rate that cannot be sustained. Alternative forms of power could light and heat more homes, with less pressure on the environment. Improved agricultural processes could grow more food with less pollution. At least a billion people do not have access to safe water, but water purification techniques could fix that.

To solve these problems, mechanical engineers will likely work with people from other disciplines. "With the expanding global population comes the need to address challenges such as clean water, sanitation, food and energy," according to the American Society of Mechanical Engineers (ASME).[3] This variety of challenges means there is plenty of work for future generations of mechanical engineers.

CONCERNS AND COMPLICATIONS

The challenges facing engineers are complex, and realistic solutions must come at a reasonable cost. Many companies will continue polluting the environment if cleaner technologies are too expensive. Some problems can be solved only with government support, yet funding is not adequate to suit current needs. For example, the current US budget for improving infrastructure falls short of estimated needs by billions of dollars.

Often compromise is required. A project's budget and schedule may prevent engineers from following some paths. Different options may affect cost, performance, reliability, and environmental impact in complex ways. Human psychology also comes into play. For example, most cars offer everything the average driver needs, so buying decisions often come down to how a car looks and feels. Thus, designing a car requires artistry as well as engineering. Market experts and consumer focus groups may have as much to do with the final design as the engineers.

DESIGNING WITH COMPUTERS

Many engineers begin work by sketching ideas on paper, as they have done for centuries. However, computers are taking over many steps of the design process. An engineer can use a computer to create a 3-D image to view a design from different angles. Software programs allow the quick creation of a cutaway drawing to reveal the inside of a mechanism. Animation shows how moving parts work together. Computer code can even predict where a design is vulnerable to stresses such as heat and electricity. All these options allow the engineer to quickly develop, share, and analyze designs. Computers also improve collaboration by allowing team members to share designs quickly, even between countries.

A BRIGHT FUTURE

Mechanical engineers believe they will be able to do their part in solving the world's problems in the coming decades. ASME surveyed more than 1,200 people working in the mechanical engineering field. The vast majority were optimistic about the engineering profession's ability to meet global challenges. ASME announced, "While the study shows optimism about the ability of engineers to meet global challenges, it points to the importance of working on interdisciplinary teams of professionals to address these issues."[4]

Engineers may also have to get training in more fields. Successful engineers will continue to learn and increase their skills. They will take advantage of the latest technologies, such as 3-D printing. These systems make it possible to quickly and cheaply transform raw materials into functional prototypes. The ability of engineers to rapidly test many prototypes has the potential to dramatically improve finished products.

The field of mechanical engineering is equal parts challenging and rewarding.

AN EDUCATED PUBLIC

The general public needs a solid understanding of engineering and science. Only people who understand the benefit of a new technology will support the laws and funding to bring it about. People are also hesitant to use technologies they do not understand, which could prevent them from taking advantage of new tools. Sometimes introducing a new technology is not enough. Engineers may also have to explain why an idea is valuable. Communication skills are key in making this happen.

The growing global marketplace will require more from engineers. Professionals put a high value on knowledge of globalization and economics. Communication skills and diplomacy are also key when it comes to working with team members around the world.

Young people who have a strong foundation in science, math, engineering, and technology are better prepared to tackle global problems. Students preparing to study engineering now will play a major part in solving these problems in the decades to come. For those with curiosity, creativity, and the desire to improve people's lives, mechanical engineering offers a future filled with possibilities.

HANDS-ON PROJECT
REVERSE ENGINEERING

One way to improve on a current product is through reverse engineering. This involves taking apart a product to analyze its structure and function. Each component may be studied individually. The goal is to find ways to duplicate or improve on the previous design. Reverse engineering involves careful observation, disassembly, documentation, analysis, and reporting.

Find a toy or machine you can take apart. Options include toy cars, dolls with movable parts, a mechanical pencil or pen, water toys, a disposable camera, or an old watch. Garage sales or secondhand stores

Even a product as small as a wristwatch can contain dozens of unique parts.

are good places to look for items. For safety reasons, avoid items that use electricity or have sharp points.

Sketch the item, labeling the parts you can see and identifying their functions. Try to picture the inside of the product. Make a diagram of how you predict the inside would look. Then, take apart the item. Sketch each part and label it. Write a brief description of what each part does.

Finally, answer the following questions:

- What does this device do? How do the parts work together to fulfill that function?

- How did the inside of the product compare with your guess?

- Are there any flaws in how the item works? How would you improve it?

- What materials were used for the parts? Why would the engineers have chosen them?

- Could the item function differently? How would you redesign it to do something else?

PLANNING A CAREER

In high school, students who wish to become mechanical engineers should focus on mathematics and science courses. A solid understanding of the scientific method is important.

In college, students should continue with science and math classes. Joining groups or clubs of mechanical engineers can help students get to know other people in their field. It is also a good idea to seek out internships in the mechanical engineering field. These give students valuable real-world engineering experience.

Most mechanical engineering jobs require a bachelor's degree in mechanical engineering. A graduate degree may be needed for managerial positions or teaching in higher education.

ESSENTIAL FACTS
CURIOSITY MARS ROVER

PROJECT DATES
Launch: November 26, 2011, 10:02 a.m. Eastern Standard Time (EST), from Cape Canaveral Air Force Station, Florida

Landing: August 6, 2012, approximately 1:31 a.m. EST, on Mars near the base of Mount Sharp inside Gale Crater

KEY PLAYERS
NASA worked with researchers from the United States, Russia, and Spain to provide the tools for the ten science investigations. Science operations and analysis are coordinated through the Mars Science Laboratory Project Science Group.

KEY TOOLS AND TECHNOLOGIES
- The innovative Sky Crane landing system carried the rover to the Martian surface.

- Autonomous navigation allows the rover to decide how to drive safely.

- A special suspension system keeps the rover steady and upright.

THE IMPACT OF THE *CURIOSITY* MARS ROVER
The *Curiosity* rover perfected a new landing technique for big payloads. It also determined that Gale Crater could have supported microbial life in the ancient past and found an ancient streambed where water once flowed. The rover and its team helped bring planetary science into the public eye.

ESSENTIAL FACTS
DA VINCI SURGICAL SYSTEM

PROJECT DATES
Animal trials began in 1996. Human trials began in 1997. Limited FDA approval was received in 1997. On July 11, 2000, the da Vinci Surgical System received FDA approval for use in all laparoscopic surgical procedures.

KEY PLAYERS
The Defense Advanced Research Projects Agency (DARPA) provided the funding that launched the robotic surgery field. The Stanford Research Institute and other research groups developed the technology. Frederic Moll founded Intuitive Surgical to produce and market the system.

KEY TOOLS AND TECHNOLOGIES
- Enlarged 3-D images help the surgeon see better.

- Multiple robot arms, which can bend and rotate more than a human wrist, can hold several different instruments.

THE IMPACT OF THE DA VINCI SURGICAL SYSTEM
The system allows the surgeon to overcome the limits of the human hand. Surgical incisions are smaller, so the patient may lose less blood and have smaller scars. Patients may recover faster with a shorter hospital stay, which saves money.

ESSENTIAL FACTS
ENERCON E-126

PROJECT DATES
A prototype of the E-126 was installed in August 2002. The second generation E-126 was introduced in 2007.

At the Estinnes, Belgium, wind farm, construction began in 2008. The first turbines became operational in 2009.

KEY PLAYERS
German engineer Aloys Wobben founded Enercon in 1984.

KEY TOOLS AND TECHNOLOGIES
- Enercon developed its own process for making concrete towers.

- A special giant crane, the largest of its type in the world, was designed and built especially to meet the needs of the E-126.

THE IMPACT OF THE E-126 WIND TURBINE
Each E-126 turbine produces enough energy to power thousands of homes. An advanced prototype version of the E-126 will be tested in high-speed winds off the coast of France.

GLOSSARY

bending
Curving due to forces that cause one part of a material to be in compression and another part to be in tension.

compression
A force that squeezes material together.

decomposition
Chemical breakdown, such as rotting or decay.

disintegration
Physical breakdown, such as cracking or breaking.

patent infringement
The manufacture or use of an invention for which someone else owns the patent without permission of the patent owner.

prototype
A working model of a product that is used for testing before final versions are manufactured.

rotor
A rotating part of a mechanical or electric device.

suspension
The system on a vehicle that keeps the vehicle level even as its wheels drive over rough terrain.

telesurgery
Surgery performed by a doctor who is not directly touching the patient, using robotics and computer technology.

tension
A force that pulls material apart; the state of being tightly stretched.

turbine
A machine with a revolving wheel or rotor, usually with blades that spin under the pressure of air, water, gas, or steam.

ADDITIONAL RESOURCES

SELECTED BIBLIOGRAPHY

Engineers. New York: DK, 2012. Print.

Lewis, E. E. *Masterworks of Technology: The Story of Creative Engineering, Architecture, and Design*. Amherst, NY: Prometheus, 2004. Print.

FURTHER READINGS

Brain, Marshall. *How Stuff Works*. Edison, NJ: Chartwell, 2008. Print.

Macaulay, David. *The New Way Things Work*. Boston, MA: Houghton Mifflin, 1998. Print.

Wiens, Roger. *Red Rover: Inside the Story of Robotic Space Exploration, from Genesis to the Mars Rover Curiosity*. New York: Basic, 2013. Print.

WEBSITES

To learn more about Great Achievements in Engineering, visit **booklinks.abdopublishing.com**. These links are routinely monitored and updated to provide the most current information available.

FOR MORE INFORMATION

For more information on this subject, contact or visit the following organizations:

Great Lakes Science Center

601 Erieside Avenue

Cleveland, OH 44114

216-694-2000

http://www.glsc.org

This museum has hundreds of hands-on science exhibits relating to light, optics, mechanics, electricity, and more, plus science demonstrations and a six-story theater. The NASA Glenn Visitor Center has exhibits on aeronautics and space exploration, including space shuttle and lunar lander models and flight simulators.

Jet Propulsion Laboratory (JPL)

4800 Oak Grove Drive

Pasadena, CA 91109

818-354-4321

http://www.jpl.nasa.gov

A research center and NASA field center, JPL offers free tours with advance reservations. A multimedia presentation provides an overview of the laboratory's accomplishments.

SOURCE NOTES

CHAPTER 1. CREATING A BETTER WORLD

1. "Chicago Native to Oversee Curiosity Landing on Mars." *CBS Chicago.* CBS Local, 5 Aug. 2012. Web. 6 Mar. 2014.

2. Dauna Coulter. "Strange but True: Curiosity's Sky Crane." *NASA Science News.* NASA, 30 July 2012. Web. 6 Mar. 2014.

3. "Curiosity's Seven Minutes of Terror." *Jet Propulsion Laboratory.* NASA, 22 June 2012. Web. 6 Mar. 2014.

4. Dauna Coulter. "Strange but True: Curiosity's Sky Crane." *NASA Science News.* NASA, 30 July 2012. Web. 6 Mar. 2014.

5. "Ultimate Mars Challenge." *Nova.* PBS, 14 Nov. 2012. Web. 6 Mar. 2014.

6. Dauna Coulter. "Strange but True: Curiosity's Sky Crane." *NASA Science News.* NASA, 30 July 2012. Web. 6 Mar. 2014.

7. "For NASA Rover Team, Many Years of Work and 'Seven Minutes of Terror' Paid Off." *PBS NewsHour.* PBS, 6 Aug. 2012. Web. 6 Mar. 2014.

8. "Trends in Mechanical Engineering Careers." *Department of Mechanical Engineering.* Stony Brook State University of New York, n.d. Web. 6 Mar. 2014.

9. "Mechanical Engineers." *Occupational Outlook Handbook.* Bureau of Labor Statistics, 8 Jan. 2014. Web. 6 Mar. 2014.

10. "Measures of Central Tendency For Wage Data." *Social Security Administration.* Social Security Administration, n.d. Web. 6 Mar. 2014.

CHAPTER 2. MECHANICAL ENGINEERING

None.

CHAPTER 3. THE ROAD TO MARS

1. William Harwood. "Curiosity Rover Drives $2.5B Make-or-Break Mars Mission." *CNET*. CNET, 31 July 2012. Web. 6 Mar. 2014.

2. "Mars Facts." *Athena Mars Exploration Rovers*. Cornell University, 2005. Web. 7 Mar. 2014.

3. "Ultimate Mars Challenge." *Nova*. PBS, 14 Nov. 2012. Web. 6 Mar. 2014.

4. Ibid.

5. "Women Talk: 10+ Questions With Rocket Scientist, Dr. Anita Sengupta." *Women You Should Know*. Outhouse PR, 27 Aug. 2013. Web. 10 Mar. 2014.

CHAPTER 4. EXPLORING THE RED PLANET

1. "Mars Science Laboratory Landing Press Kit." *NASA*. NASA, July 2012. Web. 6 Mar. 2014.

2. "Mars Facts." *NASA Quest*. NASA, n.d. Web. 6 Mar. 2014.

3. "Mars Science Laboratory Landing Press Kit." *NASA*. NASA, July 2012. Web. 6 Mar. 2014.

4. "Ultimate Mars Challenge." *Nova*. PBS, 14 Nov. 2012. Web. 6 Mar. 2014.

5. Ibid.

6. "Mars Science Laboratory/Curiosity Fact Sheet." *NASA*. NASA, Aug. 2012. Web. 6 Mar. 2014.

7. "Power." *Mars Science Laboratory Curiosity Rover*. NASA, n.d. Web. 6 Mar. 2014.

8. Thomas Ormston. "Time Delay Between Mars and Earth." *Mars Express Blog*. European Space Agency, 8 May 2012. Web. 6 Mar. 2014.

9. Guy Webster. "NASA's Mars Curiosity Debuts Autonomous Navigation." *Solar System Exploration*. NASA, 27 Aug. 2013. Web. 6 Mar. 2014.

10. William Harwood. "Curiosity Rover Drives $2.5B Make-or-Break Mars Mission." *CNET*. CNET, 31 July 2012. Web. 6 Mar. 2014.

11. Ibid.

CHAPTER 5. A ROBOT SURGEON

1. "Da Vinci Surgical System." *Robotic Surgery*. Brown University, n.d. Web. 6 Mar. 2014.

2. Barnaby J. Feder. "Prepping Robots to Perform Surgery." *New York Times*. New York Times, 4 May 2008. Web. 6 Mar. 2014.

3. Robin Eisner. "FDA OKs First Robotic Surgical Device." *ABC News*. ABC News, 13 July 2013. Web. 6 Mar. 2014.

SOURCE NOTES CONTINUED

CHAPTER 6. TROUBLESHOOTING DA VINCI

1. "Da Vinci Surgical System." *Robotic Surgery*. Brown University, n.d. Web. 6 Mar. 2014.

2. Roni Caryn Rabin. "New Concerns on Robotic Surgeries." *New York Times*. New York Times, 9 Sept. 2013. Web. 7 Mar. 2014.

3. Ibid.

4. Barnaby J. Feder. "Prepping Robots to Perform Surgery." *New York Times*. New York Times, 4 May 2008. Web. 6 Mar. 2014.

CHAPTER 7. POWER FROM THE AIR

1. Tyler Hamilton. *Mad Like Tesla: Underdog Inventors and the Relentless Pursuit of Clean Energy*. Toronto, ON: ECW, 2011. Print. 24.

2. Thomas K. Grose. "IEA World Outlook: Six Key Trends Shaping the Energy Future." *National Geographic*. National Geographic, 12 Nov. 2013. Web. 18 Nov. 2013.

3. *Marvels of Engineering*. Washington, DC: National Geographic, 2007. Print. 171–172.

4. "Energy Dept. Reports: US Wind Energy Production and Manufacturing Reaches Record Highs." *Energy.gov*. US Department of Energy, 6 Aug. 2013. Web. 7 Mar. 2014.

5. Ibid.

6. "Wind Energy." *Bureau of Land Management*. US Department of the Interior, 2 Jan. 2014. Web. 7 Mar. 2014.

7. "Energy Dept. Reports: US Wind Energy Production and Manufacturing Reaches Record Highs." *Energy.gov*. US Department of Energy, 6 Aug. 2013. Web. 7 Mar. 2014.

8. Eize de Vries. "E-126 in Action: Enercon's Next-Generation Power Plant." *RenewableEnergyWorld.com*. RenewableEnergyWorld.com, 16 Sept. 2009. Web. 7 Mar. 2014.

9. Ibid.

10. Ibid.

11. Ibid.

12. Ibid.

CHAPTER 8. KEEPING THE LIGHTS ON

1. Thomas K. Grose. "IEA World Outlook: Six Key Trends Shaping the Energy Future." *National Geographic*. National Geographic, 12 Nov. 2013. Web. 18 Nov. 2013.

2. "The Science." *Whale Power*. Whale Power, 19 Nov. 2013. Web. 7 Mar. 2014.

3. "Whale Fins Influence Wind Turbine Designs." *Windpower Engineering*. Windpower Engineering, 14 Sept. 2009. Web. 7 Mar. 2014.

4. Zachary Shahan. "GE Boosting Wind Turbine Output up to 5% with PowerUp, Industrial Internet Technology." *CleanTechnica*. Important Media, 9 Oct. 2013. Web. 7 Mar. 2014.

5. Ruth Graham. "A Turning Point for Offshore Wind Energy?" *Al Jazeera America*. Al Jazeera, 18 Nov. 2013. Web. 7 Mar. 2014.

CHAPTER 9. THE FUTURE OF ENGINEERING

1. Mark Crawford. "Engineering Still Needs More Women." *ASME*. ASME, Sept. 2012. Web. 7 Mar. 2014.

2. Ruth Graham. "Meet the 6 Amazing Women of NASA's Mars Curiosity Mission." *The Grindstone*. The Gloss, 6 Aug. 2012. Web. 7 Mar. 2014.

3. "ASME Releases Study on the Future of the Mechanical Engineering Profession." *ASME*. ASME, 2014. Web. 7 Mar. 2014.

4. David Butcher. "A Brief Look into the Future of Mechanical Engineering." *Industry Market Trends*. Thomasnet News, 11 Sept. 2012. Web. 7 Mar. 2014.

INDEX

ABOUT THE AUTHOR

Chris Eboch writes about science, history, and culture for all ages. Her novels for young people include historical fiction, ghost stories, and action-packed adventures.

ABOUT THE CONTENT CONSULTANT

Carrie Hall is an assistant professor at the Illinois Institute of Technology. She teaches mechanical engineering courses and works with students on research projects involving automotive engines.